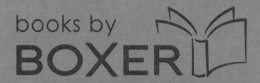

www.booksbyboxer.com

Published by
Books By Boxer, Leeds, LS13 4BS UK
Books by Boxer (EU), Dublin D02 P593 IRELAND
© Books By Boxer 2022
All Rights Reserved
MADE IN CHINA
ISBN: 9781909732971

Where does a King keep his armies?

In his sleevies!

Three blind mice walk into a bar...

...and a table, and a chair.

What's orange and sounds like a parrot?

A carrot.

What do you call a cow with no legs?

Ground beef.

What do you call an alligator in a vest?

An investigator.

What did the fish say when it hit the wall?

Dam.

Two drums and a cymbal fall off a cliff...

...ba dum tss.

What's the best time to go to the dentist?

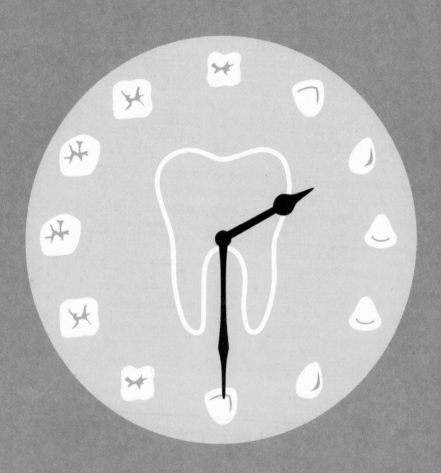

2:30.

What's the difference between roast beef and pea soup?

Anyone can roast beef.

Why can't a bike stand on its own?

It's two tyred.

Why do graveyards have gates?

Because people are dying to get in.

Why do flamingos lift up one leg?

If they lifted both, they would fall.

Why did the blind man fall into a well?

He couldn't see that well.

What do you call a wingless fly?

A walk.

I'm friends with 25 letters of the alphabet.

I don't know Y.

What's blue and not heavy?

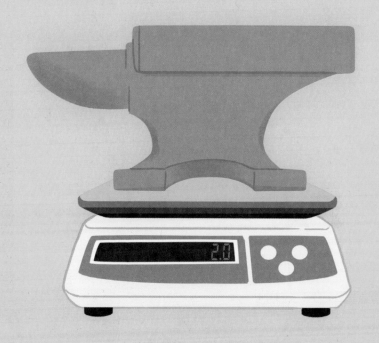

Light blue.

What do you call a computer that sings?

A dell.

How do you organise a party in space?

You planet.

What do you call a fish with no eyes?

A fsh.

What do you get when you cross a kangaroo with a sheep?

A woolly jumper.

Two goldfish are in a tank, one turns and says to the other...

"You steer and I'll man the gun."

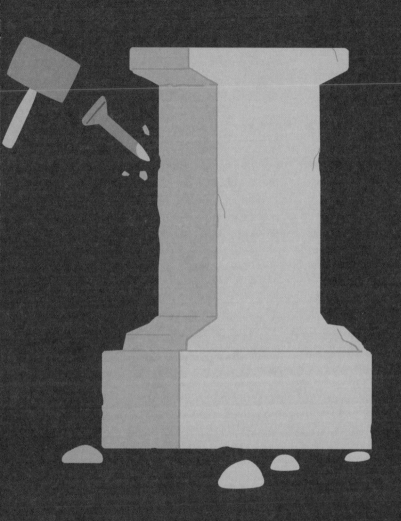

I, for one like
Roman Numerals.

What do you call a man with a rubber toe?

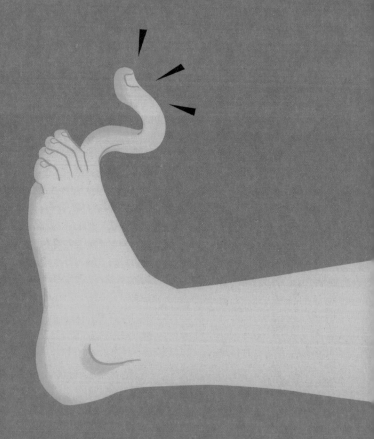

Roberto.

Did you hear the rumour about butter?

I really shouldn't be spreading it...

A termite walks into a bar and says...

"Is the bar tender here?"

Did you hear about the circus fire?

It was in tents.

My wife said I should do lunges to help keep in shape.

That would be a big step forward.

What does a tick and the Eiffel Tower have in common?

I ♥ PARIS

They're both Paris sites.

Why don't oysters share their pearls?

Because they're shellfish.

How do you make a Kleenex dance?

Put a little boogie in it.

I've got a great pizza joke for you...

KNOCK KNOCK

Never mind... It's too cheesy.

What kind of shoes do ninjas wear?

Sneak-ers.

What do you call it when Batman skips church?

Christian Bale.

How do you get a farmer girl's attention?

A tractor.

What do you call a magician that loses his magic?

Ian.

Why is Peter Pan always flying?

Because he never-lands.

Did you hear about the restaurant on the moon?

Great food, no atmosphere.

Want to hear a great joke about building?

I'm still working on it.

Where did I learn to make banana splits?

Sundae school.

What's brown and sounds like a bell?

Duuuunnnng.

When life gives you melons...

You might be dyslexic.

A girl came up to me and said she recognised me from her vegetarian restaurant....

I was a bit confused. I'd never met herbivore.

If pronouncing my b's as v's makes me sound Russian...

...then Soviet.

Why can't towels tell jokes?

They have a dry sense of humour.

How was Rome split in two?

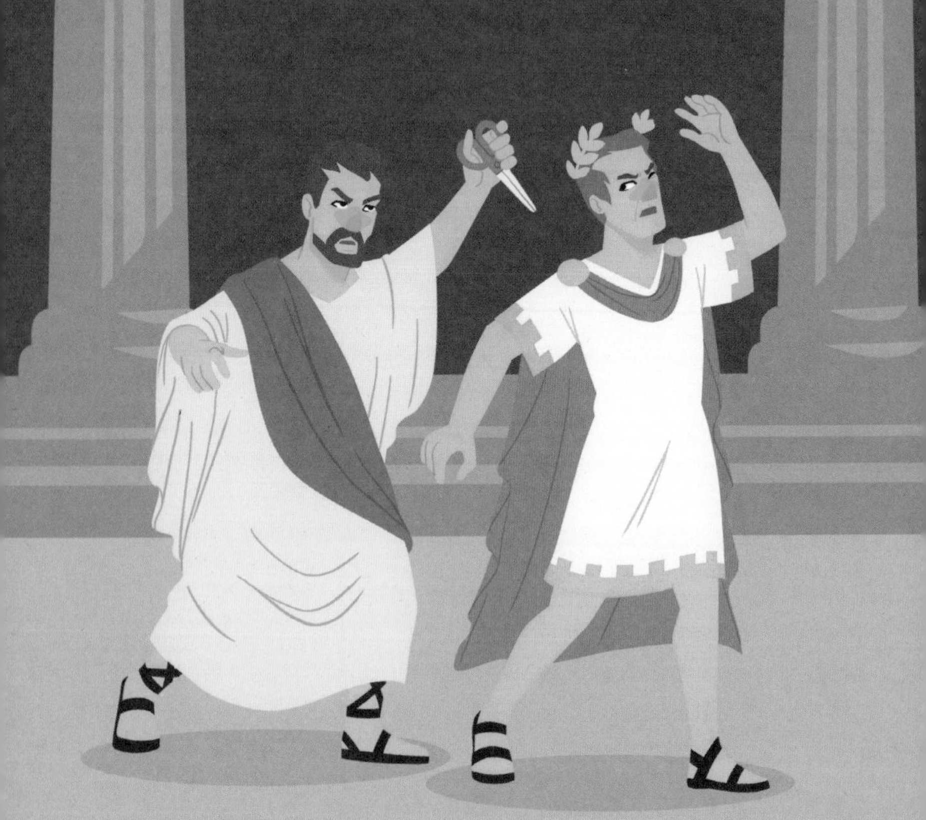

With a pair of Caesars.

Why were the utensils stuck together?

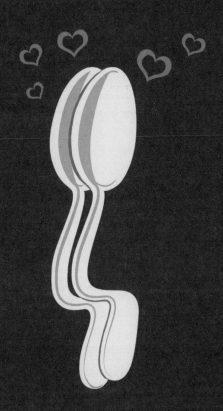

They were spooning.

Who invented King Arthur's table?

Sir Cumference.

My wife blocked me on
Facebook because I post
too many bird puns.

Well, toucan play
at that game.

I've been reading a horror story in braille. Something bad is about to happen...

...I can feel it.

I'm trying to organise a
hide-&-seek tournament.

But good players are
really hard to find.

Think swimming with dolphins is expensive? Try swimming with sharks...

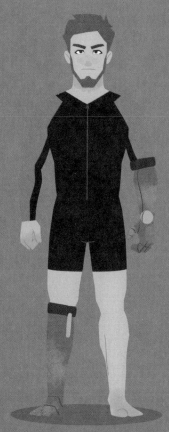

It cost me an arm and a leg.

What's the difference between a poorly dressed man on a trike and a well dressed man on a bike?

Attire.

What do you call a magic dog?

Abracalabrador.

What do you call a fish wearing a bow tie?

Sofishticated.

How does the moon cut his hair?

Eclipse it.

What's the most condescending bear?

A pan-duh.

Why do bees have sticky hair?

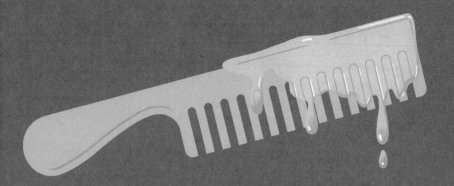

They use a honeycomb.

Did you hear about the kidnapping at school?

Its fine, he woke up.

What kind of car does an egg drive?

A Yolkswagen.

How do you make Lady Gaga angry?

Being an organ donor is so brave...

It really takes guts!

How do you row a canoe full of puppies?

Use a doggy paddle.

I had a dream that I was swimming in an ocean of orange soda...

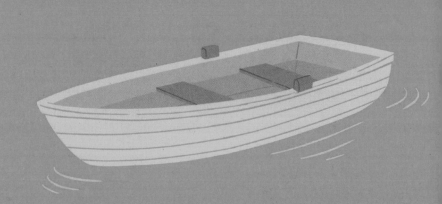

It was just a Fanta-sea.

I told my doctor that
I keep hearing a
buzzing sound.

He said that there's a
bug going round.

What did the drummer call his daughters?

Anna One, Anna Two.

What's Forrest Gump's computer password?

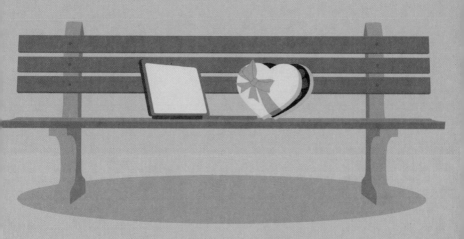

1forrest1.

What does a nosey pepper do?

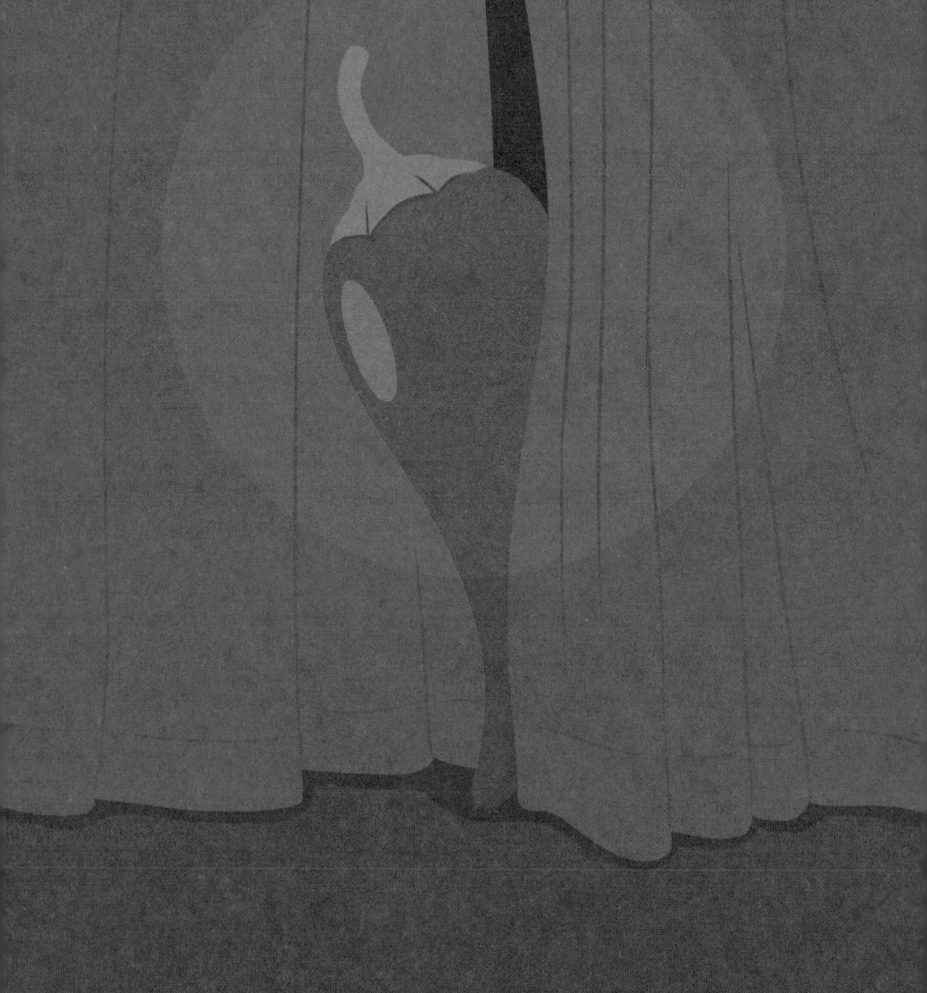

Gets jalapeño business.

R.I.P to boiling water...

You will be mist.

What do you call a fibbing cat?

A lion.

What do you call a zombie cooking a stir-fry?

Dead man wok-ing.

I was wondering why the frisbee was looking bigger and bigger...

And then it hit me.

What do you call a penguin at Buckingham Palace?

Lost.

What country's capital city is growing the fastest?

Ireland - every day it's Dublin.

What is the best smelling insect?

A Deodor-ant.

I ordered a chicken and an egg online.

I'll let you know...

Mountains aren't just funny...

They're hill areas.

Why does Snoop Dogg carry an umbrella?

Fo' Drizzle.

I just got a promotion at the farm.

I'm now the C-I-E-I-O.

What do you call a pony with a sore throat?

A little hoarse.

What do you call two monkeys that share an Amazon account?

Prime-mates.

How do you weigh a millennial?

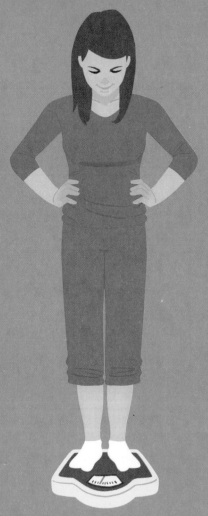

In Instagrams.

I told my girlfriend
that she drew her
eyebrows too high.

She looked surprised.

What do you call two octopuses that look the same?

Itentacle.

What does a house wear?

Address.

My wife asked me to
get 6 cans of sprite
from the shops.

I noticed when I
got home that I'd
picked 7up by mistake.

What noise does a witch's vehicle make?

Broom Broom.

My mate asked me to stop singing Oasis all the time...

...I said maybeee.

What did the pirate say on his 80th birthday?

Aye Matey.

Someone has glued my pack of cards together.

I don't know how to deal with it.

I used to be addicted to the hokey cokey.

But don't worry... I turned myself around.